This Notebook Belongs To:

If Found, Please Contact Me At:

BRIL·LIANCE

NOUN

· intense brightness of light

· exceptional talent or intelligence

Create Your Life

A Notebook for Effortless Expansion and Infinite Abundance

Created By Elysia Skye

Awesome Legal Disclaimer!

Create Your Life: A Notebook for Effortless Expansion and Infinite Abundance is a work of my own creation.

Any resemblance to actual events, locations, businesses, or persons (living or dead) are entirely coincidental unless specifically noted and credited.

The ideas and encouragements expressed in this journal do not replace the advice of a medical professional or trained therapist. Consult your physician before making any changes to your diet or regular health plan.

The information in this book was correct at the time of publication, and the Author does not assume any liability for loss or damage caused by errors or omissions, again, this is my perspective, opinion, and experience, so it has been written as such.

ISBN 978-1-961185-01-2

www.inomniaparatuspublishing.com

How To Create Your life

⚠ **WARNING**

We're about to get
WOO WOO!

The first thing you should know is that you're not doing this alone, and you never have.

You are co-creating your life with the universe, and every bit of that energy is with you, supporting you to flourish, expand, and become even more magnificent!

You might refer to this energy as your inner knowing, your higher self, your guides, your angels, or maybe your own intelligence. Whatever it is to you, listen to it unapologetically, and take action on what you're receiving.

The second thing is that by choosing to create your life, you are committed to using your unique brilliance to shape your entire life, which will inevitably have a highly positive impact on others.

By shining your light you give other people permission to do the same. So thank you for being a trailblazer. The world needs more people like you.

And the third and final thing that you must do during heightened periods of creativity is REST.

When I am in "mad scientist mode", creating like a wild woman, I feel like time stands still, I sometimes forget to eat, and I don't like being interrupted to do daily tasks. I just want to create.

What you're about to experience is the thrilling momentum of creativity in action! However, if you don't take proper breaks, eat nourishing meals, and sleep deeply, you will burn out. Don't do that.

There is nothing sexy about suffering just to prove you accomplished something. Trust me! Been there, done that from 1994 to 2005.

Spoiler alert: It didn't end very well, which I'll tell you more about in a few pages.

You are not a machine. You are an organic and energetic being. You deserve to rest. Rest is recharging your system for even better ideas to come.

How To Use This Notebook

Every few pages you will come across an inspired quote by someone who has created their life.

These are magic makers, trailblazers, and people who don't ask for permission to be great! They follow their heart, knowing the destination is worth the journey.

After the thought provoking quote, you'll receive additional guidance on how to create what's next for you, followed by an action-taking prompt.

Listen to your intuition and create mindful minutes to consciously consider what's being asked of you.

And here's the deal...

Even if you just use this notebook for to-do lists, taking notes during coaching sessions, or to test out your new glitter pens, it is YOURS.

You know what else is yours? Your entire life.

Claim it.

Infinite abundance is your birthright. This is why I give my Brilliance Method Sapphire Collective clients this gold coin necklace.

WHO AM I?

Course Creator & Producer

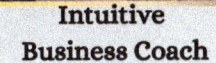

Intuitive Business Coach

Author, Speaker & Host

I am creative.

Creativity is a part of everything I do and how I see the world. I was born this way. Even in business, my creativity mixed with my intuition has been the #1 reason I'm so successful, happy, and fulfilled.

I am love.

Love IS the energy of infinite abundance and effortless expansion. Through love all things are possible. Everything I do, I do with love as the foundation.

I am intuitive.

You are also intuitive. We all are. I grew up with an intuitive mother who nurtured this sense in me since I was little. I am so grateful that I learned to listen to my intuition and take action on behalf of what I hear and feel.

Listening to my intuition literally saved my life when I had stage 3 breast cancer at 24 years old. My doctor told me it was a cyst. Had I listened to her I would have been dead in a month. Trust yourself, always. I do.

I am a healer.

I was put on this earth to bring healing to others in many different ways.

I am privileged to be able to help other people shift their energy and perspective so that they can create their life.

I'm also hilarious (just ask me), and laughter is the best medicine of all, right?!

I am generosity.

If I've got it, I want you to have it too. If you've got it, I want to help you create more of it so that you can share it with others.

The Brilliance Method has been a blessing that is beyond welcome. Elysia's kind yet accountable approach is not only appreciated it is inspiring. I'm so thankful for the guidance and all the tips and tricks this program has offered me! It is a community of generosity, badassery and all around magic. 💜✨

Love · Reply · 55m

❤ 1

This past year was an absolute game changer in my life. Then after joining Elysia's program it has literally changed how I do business. I show up everywhere. In person I tell everyone I can about my business. I did one summit and I did a speaking slot today in someone's group. I have more in the works and I am putting together how I want my Business to run in a way that will create an evergreen buy in.

It feels so good to be this confidence again! I see myself shining more each day the way I used to shine when I was in real estate! That is exactly how I made a million in real estate! By shining.. By not hiding! By being absolutely confident In what I know I can do!!

I found it again Elysia Skye And you can totally use this as a testimonial! Thank you so much!! I am crying writing this because it means that much to me.

The money is great but that's not the point. It's so much more. It's completely the ability to shine again! 🧡💛🧡💛

I am a lighthouse.

I am not the "lifesaver". I will not jump into the dark, freezing water to pull you out.

My job is to stand strong, tall, and shine my light until you find your way, even if you're worried about what's behind you, in front of you, underneath you or above you.

I will remind you that you are safe, and guide the way for you as you keep going. We're in this together.

I hope this inspires you to always *"Be the lighthouse, not the lifesaver."*

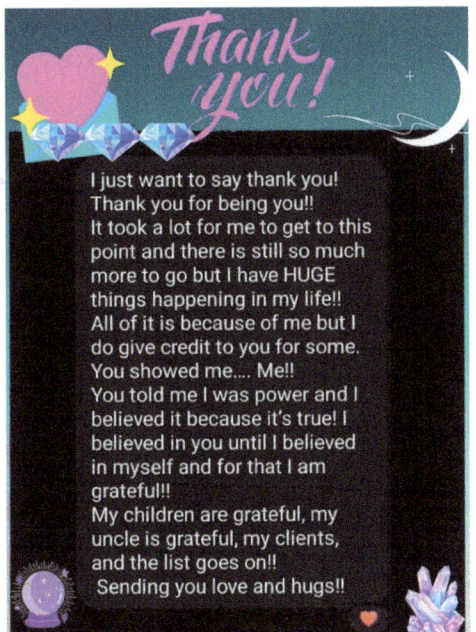

I just want to say thank you! Thank you for being you!! It took a lot for me to get to this point and there is still so much more to go but I have HUGE things happening in my life!! All of it is because of me but I do give credit to you for some. You showed me.... Me!! You told me I was power and I believed it because it's true! I believed in you until I believed in myself and for that I am grateful!! My children are grateful, my uncle is grateful, my clients, and the list goes on!! Sending you love and hugs!!

Sharing good news - after Elysia did the FB live about prices for her course, I decided to stop giving a lower price option and just offer two options - a year for $10k or 6 months for $5k. I had a sales call a day later and offered that and they said yes with monthly payments of $1k. Not even blinking or batting an eye!!

Own it ladies! You are worth it. What you offer is worth it!

Elysia... you're literally an angel that has fallen from heaven. I'm so lucky to know you and to have had the opportunity to learn more about myself with you and through you. You just make it so easy to dig deep and love myself in ways that I never have. Thank you for that gift.

LET'S CONNECT

The universe has a great plan to bring us together.

I want to know who YOU are, so pop into my facebook group, let's connect, and tell me all about you so that I can help illuminate your path as you create your life.

facebook.com/groups/trailblazercommunity

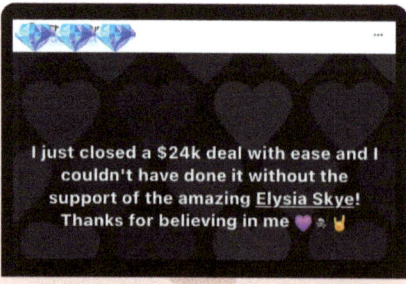

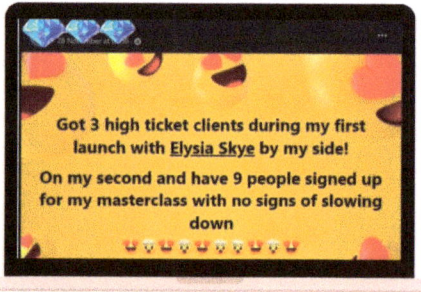

QUICK TIP

In my signature intuitive business coaching program, The Brilliance Method, we do co-working accountability "Get Shit Done" sessions (or GSD's).

To properly GSD here is what you must commit to doing:

- Communicate with the people who rely on you that you'll be unavailable. This is for them just as much as it is for you.
- Set an intention at the top of each session.
- Stay focused on one thing that you're going to accomplish during the session.
- Drink water (stay hydrated and have water nearby).
- When on Zoom with others, keep your camera on to reduce getting distracted. Knowing you are visible helps you stay focused.
- Stopping for TEN minutes every FIFTY minutes. We do fifty minutes on, and ten minutes off. No exceptions.

READY?! Let's GSD and Create Your Life!

> ## What's the ONE Thing I can do, such that by doing it, everything else will be easier or unnecessary?
> - Gary Keller -
> *The 1 Thing*

When you're creating your life, you might start off with a massive to-do list. From now on, let's infuse some magic into it and create a **ta-da list!**

Create Imperfect Action

Write your entire ta-da list of everything you have to do to create what's next in your life.

Your list can be specific to a project or situation.

Once you've written it out, circle or highlight ONE THING (and one thing only) that if you just do that one thing, it will help move everything else forward.

THEN do that one thing. Repeat this process for yourself every single day and watch your dreams manifest into reality.

JAN✿FEB✿MAR✿APR✿MAY✿JUN✿JUL✿AUG✿SEP✿OCT✿NOV✿DEC

1-2-3-4-5-6-7-8-9-10-11-12-13-14-15-16-17-18-19-20-21-22-23-24-25-26-27-28-29-30-31

JAN✲FEB✲MAR✲APR✲MAY✲JUN✲JUL✲AUG✲SEP✲OCT✲NOV✲DEC

1-2-3-4-5-6-7-8-9-10-11-12-13-14-15-16-17-18-19-20-21-22-23-24-25-26-27-28-29-30-31

JAN✵FEB✵MAR✵APR✵MAY✵JUN✵JUL✵AUG✵SEP✵OCT✵NOV✵DEC

1-2-3-4-5-6-7-8-9-10-11-12-13-14-15-16-17-18-19-20-21-22-23-24-25-26-27-28-29-30-31

JAN✣FEB✣MAR✣APR✣MAY✣JUN✣JUL✣AUG✣SEP✣OCT✣NOV✣DEC

1-2-3-4-5-6-7-8-9-10-11-12-13-14-15-16-17-18-19-20-21-22-23-24-25-26-27-28-29-30-31

> ## You don't know what you don't know. But you know more than you think you know.
> ### - Elysia Skye -

The top CEOs in the USA read an average of sixty books a year. This is because knowledge makes us unstoppable and sets us apart from those unwilling to learn.

Create Imperfect Action

Learn something new every day, starting with today.

You might choose to look something up online, or pick up a book that's been on your shelf for a while.

When I first heard this idea, I posted in the Trailblazer Community and asked everyone to share a fun fact that they've verified.

It's so much fun to learn new things, and what you learn will continue to inspire you.

JAN☆FEB☆MAR☆APR☆MAY☆JUN☆JUL☆AUG☆SEP☆OCT☆NOV☆DEC

1-2-3-4-5-6-7-8-9-10-11-12-13-14-15-16-17-18-19-20-21-22-23-24-25-26-27-28-29-30-31

JAN❅FEB❅MAR❅APR❅MAY❅JUN❅JUL❅AUG❅SEP❅OCT❅NOV❅DEC

1-2-3-4-5-6-7-8-9-10-11-12-13-14-15-16-17-18-19-20-21-22-23-24-25-26-27-28-29-30-31

JAN✦FEB✦MAR✦APR✦MAY✦JUN✦JUL✦AUG✦SEP✦OCT✦NOV✦DEC

1-2-3-4-5-6-7-8-9-10-11-12-13-14-15-16-17-18-19-20-21-22-23-24-25-26-27-28-29-30-31

JAN✣FEB✣MAR✣APR✣MAY✣JUN✣JUL✣AUG✣SEP✣OCT✣NOV✣DEC
1-2-3-4-5-6-7-8-9-10-11-12-13-14-15-16-17-18-19-20-21-22-23-24-25-26-27-28-29-30-31

JAN❊FEB❊MAR❊APR❊MAY❊JUN❊JUL❊AUG❊SEP❊OCT❊NOV❊DEC

1-2-3-4-5-6-7-8-9-10-11-12-13-14-15-16-17-18-19-20-21-22-23-24-25-26-27-28-29-30-31

Keep track of the good things people say about you in a "kudos" file.
- Sonya Sigler-
Welcome To The Next Level

On a scale from 1-10 how good are you at receiving a compliment?

Do you breathe it in and say, "thank you!" or do you toss it back and tell the other person that they've made a mistake?
THEM: *Your makeup looks great!*
YOU: *No, I did it in the car on the way here.*

I hope you'll choose to fully receive praise from now on, but this starts with you fully accepting that you are fabulous!

Create Imperfect Action

Post online (or send an email or texts) asking your community to please share what they appreciate about you.

✓ YES, you can say your coach is making you do this.

✓ YES you will survive.

And as Sonya Sigler suggests, save these notes. This will help you remember how magnificent you are. They will come in handy when you're asking for a raise or increasing your prices. When you know your value and act on it, others will too.

JAN ❋ FEB ❋ MAR ❋ APR ❋ MAY ❋ JUN ❋ JUL ❋ AUG ❋ SEP ❋ OCT ❋ NOV ❋ DEC

1-2-3-4-5-6-7-8-9-10-11-12-13-14-15-16-17-18-19-20-21-22-23-24-25-26-27-28-29-30-31

JAN✲FEB✲MAR✲APR✲MAY✲JUN✲JUL✲AUG✲SEP✲OCT✲NOV✲DEC

1-2-3-4-5-6-7-8-9-10-11-12-13-14-15-16-17-18-19-20-21-22-23-24-25-26-27-28-29-30-31

JAN✻FEB✻MAR✻APR✻MAY✻JUN✻JUL✻AUG✻SEP✻OCT✻NOV✻DEC

1-2-3-4-5-6-7-8-9-10-11-12-13-14-15-16-17-18-19-20-21-22-23-24-25-26-27-28-29-30-31

Be gentle with yourself as you transform.
- Cindy Yantis -

Transformation is defined as "a thorough or dramatic change in form or appearance".

Create Imperfect Action

Sometimes we're in the midst of a transformation and we don't even realize it because we've been in survival mode.

Pause and reflect on the last time you went through a big change in how you think, feel, or look.

Where are you now?

What do you imagine or hope this next phase of your life will result in?

Most importantly, how will your actions and intentions help create what you're imagining, versus just being caught up in circumstance?

JAN✤FEB✤MAR✤APR✤MAY✤JUN✤JUL✤AUG✤SEP✤OCT✤NOV✤DEC

1-2-3-4-5-6-7-8-9-10-11-12-13-14-15-16-17-18-19-20-21-22-23-24-25-26-27-28-29-30-31

JAN✲FEB✲MAR✲APR✲MAY✲JUN✲JUL✲AUG✲SEP✲OCT✲NOV✲DEC

1-2-3-4-5-6-7-8-9-10-11-12-13-14-15-16-17-18-19-20-21-22-23-24-25-26-27-28-29-30-31

JAN✦FEB✦MAR✦APR✦MAY✦JUN✦JUL✦AUG✦SEP✦OCT✦NOV✦DEC

1-2-3-4-5-6-7-8-9-10-11-12-13-14-15-16-17-18-19-20-21-22-23-24-25-26-27-28-29-30-31

JAN✣FEB✣MAR✣APR✣MAY✣JUN✣JUL✣AUG✣SEP✣OCT✣NOV✣DEC

1-2-3-4-5-6-7-8-9-10-11-12-13-14-15-16-17-18-19-20-21-22-23-24-25-26-27-28-29-30-31

Don't rush. Do it right.
- Elysia Skye -

The art of excellence is built on the foundation of mindfulness. When we rush, we're not in our excellence. We're mindfully missing steps and making mini messes to clean up later.
When we "do it right" the first time, we save time.

Create Imperfect Action

Begin noticing where you're moving quickly but not as efficiently.

Which areas of your life and business are being effected by this behavior?

Commit to slowing down and doing each task with *excellence.*

As soon as you begin to be aware of where you're rushing and skipping steps, you won't be able to un-know it and you'll be motivated to do your best next time.
This is NOT perfectionism.

It doesn't have to be done perfectly to be done right.

JAN✤FEB✤MAR✤APR✤MAY✤JUN✤JUL✤AUG✤SEP✤OCT✤NOV✤DEC

1-2-3-4-5-6-7-8-9-10-11-12-13-14-15-16-17-18-19-20-21-22-23-24-25-26-27-28-29-30-31

JAN☆FEB☆MAR☆APR☆MAY☆JUN☆JUL☆AUG☆SEP☆OCT☆NOV☆DEC

1-2-3-4-5-6-7-8-9-10-11-12-13-14-15-16-17-18-19-20-21-22-23-24-25-26-27-28-29-30-31

JAN⚜FEB⚜MAR⚜APR⚜MAY⚜JUN⚜JUL⚜AUG⚜SEP⚜OCT⚜NOV⚜DEC

1-2-3-4-5-6-7-8-9-10-11-12-13-14-15-16-17-18-19-20-21-22-23-24-25-26-27-28-29-30-31

I've noticed that the only times in my life I resent anything is when I've had a requirement that wasn't met.

I get to take 100% responsibility for either not communicating this requirement clearly, or not walking away sooner when it wasn't being honored.

Create Imperfect Action

Write out your list of requirements.

What do you require from your friends?

What do you require from your partner?

What do you require from your clients?

When potential clients book a Clarity Call with me I ask them what they require from their coach. If I can't meet the requirements I cancel the session and let them know why. This rarely happens since I do such a good job at attracting "my people," but I know that if we can't meet each other's requirements it won't be a match.

JAN✿FEB✿MAR✿APR✿MAY✿JUN✿JUL✿AUG✿SEP✿OCT✿NOV✿DEC

1-2-3-4-5-6-7-8-9-10-11-12-13-14-15-16-17-18-19-20-21-22-23-24-25-26-27-28-29-30-31

JAN ❖ FEB ❖ MAR ❖ APR ❖ MAY ❖ JUN ❖ JUL ❖ AUG ❖ SEP ❖ OCT ❖ NOV ❖ DEC
1-2-3-4-5-6-7-8-9-10-11-12-13-14-15-16-17-18-19-20-21-22-23-24-25-26-27-28-29-30-31

JAN✼FEB✼MAR✼APR✼MAY✼JUN✼JUL✼AUG✼SEP✼OCT✼NOV✼DEC

1-2-3-4-5-6-7-8-9-10-11-12-13-14-15-16-17-18-19-20-21-22-23-24-25-26-27-28-29-30-31

Fuck off fully, and commit fully!
- Elysia Skye -

You can't be "almost" all in and accomplish your deepest desires. When you're in, be in. When you're out, be out. The in-between invites procrastination and self-doubt.

Create Imperfect Action

Which areas of your life are you not fully committed to?

Why not?

Which ones can you release completely or delegate the tasks associated with them out to others?

These steps will invite peace into your life so that you can take real time off and feel safe to "fuck of fully" from your obligations and enjoy your days off.

Start planning your next vacation!

JAN✣FEB✣MAR✣APR✣MAY✣JUN✣JUL✣AUG✣SEP✣OCT✣NOV✣DEC

1-2-3-4-5-6-7-8-9-10-11-12-13-14-15-16-17-18-19-20-21-22-23-24-25-26-27-28-29-30-31

JAN❖FEB❖MAR❖APR❖MAY❖JUN❖JUL❖AUG❖SEP❖OCT❖NOV❖DEC
1-2-3-4-5-6-7-8-9-10-11-12-13-14-15-16-17-18-19-20-21-22-23-24-25-26-27-28-29-30-31

JAN❉FEB❉MAR❉APR❉MAY❉JUN❉JUL❉AUG❉SEP❉OCT❉NOV❉DEC

1-2-3-4-5-6-7-8-9-10-11-12-13-14-15-16-17-18-19-20-21-22-23-24-25-26-27-28-29-30-31

JAN✻FEB✻MAR✻APR✻MAY✻JUN✻JUL✻AUG✻SEP✻OCT✻NOV✻DEC

1-2-3-4-5-6-7-8-9-10-11-12-13-14-15-16-17-18-19-20-21-22-23-24-25-26-27-28-29-30-31

It's OK for it to be easy.

- Carla-Jayne Hollingworth -

In my 20's and early 30's I had a practice of making things harder on myself so that I could feel more accomplished once I completed the task. Like, I earned it or deserved it more or something. It's a lie. You can feel just as fulfilled and accomplished when something is easy and goes smoothly.

Create Imperfect Action

Revisit your ta-da list and notice where you could shorten certain steps and tasks.

How will you make things easier on yourself now?

How else will you make things easier on yourself moving forward?

Spend a few minutes in meditation, tuning into the energy of feeling worthy and deserving of ease.

JAN✳FEB✳MAR✳APR✳MAY✳JUN✳JUL✳AUG✳SEP✳OCT✳NOV✳DEC

1-2-3-4-5-6-7-8-9-10-11-12-13-14-15-16-17-18-19-20-21-22-23-24-25-26-27-28-29-30-31

JAN✲FEB✲MAR✲APR✲MAY✲JUN✲JUL✲AUG✲SEP✲OCT✲NOV✲DEC

1-2-3-4-5-6-7-8-9-10-11-12-13-14-15-16-17-18-19-20-21-22-23-24-25-26-27-28-29-30-31

> # It always works out if you let it.
> ## - Elysia Skye -

There is power in surrender. As a recovering control freak, I have to maintain intentionality on just letting things be. It's possible that the only control we have over anything is how we choose to perceive the situation.

Create Imperfect Action

Where will you invite trust, faith and surrender into your life?

Reflect back on something you worried about that worked out just fine.

Then reflect on three more situations where you worried a whole bunch but it worked out.

Notice that 99% of the things you worry about don't happen.

JAN✻FEB✻MAR✻APR✻MAY✻JUN✻JUL✻AUG✻SEP✻OCT✻NOV✻DEC

1-2-3-4-5-6-7-8-9-10-11-12-13-14-15-16-17-18-19-20-21-22-23-24-25-26-27-28-29-30-31

JAN ❖ FEB ❖ MAR ❖ APR ❖ MAY ❖ JUN ❖ JUL ❖ AUG ❖ SEP ❖ OCT ❖ NOV ❖ DEC

1-2-3-4-5-6-7-8-9-10-11-12-13-14-15-16-17-18-19-20-21-22-23-24-25-26-27-28-29-30-31

JAN❖FEB❖MAR❖APR❖MAY❖JUN❖JUL❖AUG❖SEP❖OCT❖NOV❖DEC

1-2-3-4-5-6-7-8-9-10-11-12-13-14-15-16-17-18-19-20-21-22-23-24-25-26-27-28-29-30-31

JAN✿FEB✿MAR✿APR✿MAY✿JUN✿JUL✿AUG✿SEP✿OCT✿NOV✿DEC
1-2-3-4-5-6-7-8-9-10-11-12-13-14-15-16-17-18-19-20-21-22-23-24-25-26-27-28-29-30-31

JAN✿FEB✿MAR✿APR✿MAY✿JUN✿JUL✿AUG✿SEP✿OCT✿NOV✿DEC

1-2-3-4-5-6-7-8-9-10-11-12-13-14-15-16-17-18-19-20-21-22-23-24-25-26-27-28-29-30-31

> # Don't get so busy making a living that you forget to make a life.
> ## - Dolly Parton -

Some of us live to work with no plans to retire because we love what we do. This doesn't mean that we skip out on all the magic that being human has to offer.

Create Imperfect Action

What's on your "bucket list"?
You're never too young or mature to write one or update an older version.

Use the next few pages to write out every big dream that you have.

When you're done, review it and challenge yourself to dream even bigger!

Then add at least one more.

JAN✿FEB✿MAR✿APR✿MAY✿JUN✿JUL✿AUG✿SEP✿OCT✿NOV✿DEC

1-2-3-4-5-6-7-8-9-10-11-12-13-14-15-16-17-18-19-20-21-22-23-24-25-26-27-28-29-30-31

JAN❅FEB❅MAR❅APR❅MAY❅JUN❅JUL❅AUG❅SEP❅OCT❅NOV❅DEC

1-2-3-4-5-6-7-8-9-10-11-12-13-14-15-16-17-18-19-20-21-22-23-24-25-26-27-28-29-30-31

JAN✲FEB✲MAR✲APR✲MAY✲JUN✲JUL✲AUG✲SEP✲OCT✲NOV✲DEC

1-2-3-4-5-6-7-8-9-10-11-12-13-14-15-16-17-18-19-20-21-22-23-24-25-26-27-28-29-30-31

JAN✼FEB✼MAR✼APR✼MAY✼JUN✼JUL✼AUG✼SEP✼OCT✼NOV✼DEC

1-2-3-4-5-6-7-8-9-10-11-12-13-14-15-16-17-18-19-20-21-22-23-24-25-26-27-28-29-30-31

> **I am here to receive today. I am open to everything and attached to nothing. My receiving is for my highest good, and the highest good for all in the universe. I am here to receive today. This or something greater.**
> - Elysia Skye -

This mantra has helped me with my intention setting, relationships, health, money mindset and manifestation, and just about everything that a human might fixate on to receive. This helps me create and detach.

Create Imperfect Action

Your gratitude list is directly connected to the results you have in your life.

Write nine things you're thankful for.

When you're done, notice that each thing is something to be proud of, that other people (not all but many) wish they had some of this magic in their lives too.

Then, notice that your entire list is proof that you are abundant and safe.

Even if you haven't always been or felt abundant and safe, you are right now.

You get to choose to receive in every area your life with every new choice you make.

JAN❊FEB❊MAR❊APR❊MAY❊JUN❊JUL❊AUG❊SEP❊OCT❊NOV❊DEC

1-2-3-4-5-6-7-8-9-10-11-12-13-14-15-16-17-18-19-20-21-22-23-24-25-26-27-28-29-30-31

JAN✣FEB✣MAR✣APR✣MAY✣JUN✣JUL✣AUG✣SEP✣OCT✣NOV✣DEC
1-2-3-4-5-6-7-8-9-10-11-12-13-14-15-16-17-18-19-20-21-22-23-24-25-26-27-28-29-30-31

JAN✿FEB✿MAR✿APR✿MAY✿JUN✿JUL✿AUG✿SEP✿OCT✿NOV✿DEC

1-2-3-4-5-6-7-8-9-10-11-12-13-14-15-16-17-18-19-20-21-22-23-24-25-26-27-28-29-30-31

JAN✤FEB✤MAR✤APR✤MAY✤JUN✤JUL✤AUG✤SEP✤OCT✤NOV✤DEC

1-2-3-4-5-6-7-8-9-10-11-12-13-14-15-16-17-18-19-20-21-22-23-24-25-26-27-28-29-30-31

JAN✿FEB✿MAR✿APR✿MAY✿JUN✿JUL✿AUG✿SEP✿OCT✿NOV✿DEC

1-2-3-4-5-6-7-8-9-10-11-12-13-14-15-16-17-18-19-20-21-22-23-24-25-26-27-28-29-30-31

JAN✳FEB✳MAR✳APR✳MAY✳JUN✳JUL✳AUG✳SEP✳OCT✳NOV✳DEC

1-2-3-4-5-6-7-8-9-10-11-12-13-14-15-16-17-18-19-20-21-22-23-24-25-26-27-28-29-30-31

> ## The truth is, we are all basically the universe—pretending to be humans for a brief moment of time.
> ### - RuPaul Charles -

The ONLY things that actually matter aren't things at all, but rather, love, forgiveness and compassion.

Create Imperfect Action

Consider for a brief moment or two that YOU are not separated from universal love and oneness.

You are connected to the entire universe, which includes every person you know, have known, and will ever know.

Write three things that if you fully forgave and released them, you would create more peace and space in your life.

No conversations need to be had. You can simply just let it go. Inhale and exhale love.

JAN❖FEB❖MAR❖APR❖MAY❖JUN❖JUL❖AUG❖SEP❖OCT❖NOV❖DEC

1-2-3-4-5-6-7-8-9-10-11-12-13-14-15-16-17-18-19-20-21-22-23-24-25-26-27-28-29-30-31

JAN✣FEB✣MAR✣APR✣MAY✣JUN✣JUL✣AUG✣SEP✣OCT✣NOV✣DEC

1-2-3-4-5-6-7-8-9-10-11-12-13-14-15-16-17-18-19-20-21-22-23-24-25-26-27-28-29-30-31

JAN✻FEB✻MAR✻APR✻MAY✻JUN✻JUL✻AUG✻SEP✻OCT✻NOV✻DEC

1-2-3-4-5-6-7-8-9-10-11-12-13-14-15-16-17-18-19-20-21-22-23-24-25-26-27-28-29-30-31

JAN✲FEB✲MAR✲APR✲MAY✲JUN✲JUL✲AUG✲SEP✲OCT✲NOV✲DEC

1-2-3-4-5-6-7-8-9-10-11-12-13-14-15-16-17-18-19-20-21-22-23-24-25-26-27-28-29-30-31

JAN✤FEB✤MAR✤APR✤MAY✤JUN✤JUL✤AUG✤SEP✤OCT✤NOV✤DEC

1-2-3-4-5-6-7-8-9-10-11-12-13-14-15-16-17-18-19-20-21-22-23-24-25-26-27-28-29-30-31

JAN❀FEB❀MAR❀APR❀MAY❀JUN❀JUL❀AUG❀SEP❀OCT❀NOV❀DEC

1-2-3-4-5-6-7-8-9-10-11-12-13-14-15-16-17-18-19-20-21-22-23-24-25-26-27-28-29-30-31

> ## True abundance is waking up every day and only doing what you feel motivated and inspired to do.
> ### - Elysia Skye -

Even though at this point in my life I get to do whatever I want to do most of the time, there are still things that need to be done that don't thrill me, like the dishes.

I may not feel a personal desire to do them, but I want the result that doing the dishes provides (the clean dishes and sink). When taking action on behalf of true abundance, it doesn't mean you love doing each thing, but you do love the end result.

Create Imperfect Action

Design your perfect day, from morning to night.

Once you've written it out, begin implementing as many things from it as possible right away, even if it's one thing at a time.

You are infinite abundance.

JAN ❖ FEB ❖ MAR ❖ APR ❖ MAY ❖ JUN ❖ JUL ❖ AUG ❖ SEP ❖ OCT ❖ NOV ❖ DEC

1-2-3-4-5-6-7-8-9-10-11-12-13-14-15-16-17-18-19-20-21-22-23-24-25-26-27-28-29-30-31

JAN✻FEB✻MAR✻APR✻MAY✻JUN✻JUL✻AUG✻SEP✻OCT✻NOV✻DEC

1-2-3-4-5-6-7-8-9-10-11-12-13-14-15-16-17-18-19-20-21-22-23-24-25-26-27-28-29-30-31

JAN✿FEB✿MAR✿APR✿MAY✿JUN✿JUL✿AUG✿SEP✿OCT✿NOV✿DEC

1-2-3-4-5-6-7-8-9-10-11-12-13-14-15-16-17-18-19-20-21-22-23-24-25-26-27-28-29-30-31

JAN✻FEB✻MAR✻APR✻MAY✻JUN✻JUL✻AUG✻SEP✻OCT✻NOV✻DEC
1-2-3-4-5-6-7-8-9-10-11-12-13-14-15-16-17-18-19-20-21-22-23-24-25-26-27-28-29-30-31

JAN❉FEB❉MAR❉APR❉MAY❉JUN❉JUL❉AUG❉SEP❉OCT❉NOV❉DEC

1-2-3-4-5-6-7-8-9-10-11-12-13-14-15-16-17-18-19-20-21-22-23-24-25-26-27-28-29-30-31

In Gratitude

With every inhale, choose to breathe in LOVE.

With every exhale, choose to breathe out LOVE.

This is the truth of who you are, and by mindfully choosing intentions with your breath, you get to share your creativity with the world.

That is a form of generosity. So if you feel inclined to hide or keep your magic hidden from others... stop it.

You are here to be seen, to be heard, and to make an impact for the greater good.

My wish is that this notebook continues to illuminate the generous, loving, intuitive, creative, empowered, brilliant being that you are.

You are worthy and deserving of a happy life.

And no matter how far along you are on your journey, this next chapter is just beginning.

XO,

Elysia Skye

Create Your Life: A Notebook for Effortless Expansion and Infinite Abundance, is dedicated to the women who raised me to become the woman I am.

Thank you to my mother, Jaime Lee, my sister, Arielle, my grandmother, Jeanette, my godmother, Vivienne, and my aunt, Rachel.

You continue to be the beacon of light I look to when I require help finding my way.

I love you.

Check out my other books, and audiobooks available on Amazon.

My linktree has all current resources.

https://linktr.ee/elysiaskye

www.ingramcontent.com/pod-product-compliance
Lightning Source LLC
Chambersburg PA
CBHW051528120626
46551CB00012B/1133